HOW TO WIN AT CHESS

BY GRANDMASTER
DANIEL KING

KINGFISHER
LONDON & NEW YORK

Text copyright © Daniel King 2000, 2023
Copyright © Macmillan Publishers International Ltd 2000, 2023
First American edition published in 2000
This updated edition published in 2023 in the United States by Kingfisher
120 Broadway, New York, NY 10271

Distributed in the U.S. and Canada by Macmillan.
120 Broadway, New York, NY 10271

Author: Daniel King

2023 edition:
Design: Jake Da'Costa, Amelia Brooks, Lisa Sodeau
Editor: Elizabeth Yeates

ISBN: 978-0-7534-7828-8

Kingfisher books are available for special promotions and premiums.
For details contact: Special Markets Department, Macmillan,
120 Broadway, New York, NY 10271.

For more information, please visit www.kingfisherbooks.com

EU representative: Macmillan Publishers Ireland Limited, 1st Floor,
The Liffey Trust Centre, 117-126 Sheriff Street Upper, Dublin 1, D01 YC43

A CIP catalogue record for this book is available from the British Library.

Printed in China
9 8 7 6 5 4 3
3TR/0923/WKT/UG/128MA

MIX
Paper | Supporting
responsible forestry
FSC
www.fsc.org
FSC® C116313

CONTENTS

INTRODUCTION

The Isle of Lewis chess pieces date back to about the 1100s. They form the oldest surviving complete set.

Chess is a game of war. You control one army and your opponent, the enemy, controls the other. The fate of your army depends entirely on your own skill.

Most other games rely on chance—a move may be determined by the roll of a dice, or the turn of a card. But in chess there is no luck. You are entirely responsible for your own success or failure, and this is why chess can be one of the most satisfying of all games to win.

THE ULTIMATE GAME

Before you make a move on the chessboard you must try to predict, as far as you can, how your opponent will react. In deciding what to play, you will need to use reason, memory, and logic combined with a dash of intuition and inspiration.

It has been claimed that there are more possible moves on the chessboard than the number of atoms in the universe. This helps account for the game's popularity through the ages. Chess has never been "solved." Even in today's computer age, it remains as complex and fascinating as it must have been when it emerged in India, almost 1,500 years ago.

The ancient game of chess has developed into one of the world's most popular online esports.

From the 700s until the 1000s, the Islamic world produced the best chess players. The Arabs were the first players to record their moves. Many of these games survive to this day.

THE ORIGINS OF CHESS

No one knows how the game of chess began. It is not clear whether it was invented by one person, or whether several different games gradually merged into one. Board games have been played for at least 6,000 years, but the game we recognize as chess can be traced back to 7th-century India. Its roots probably go back further. The game may even have emerged from a religious ceremony held in order to divine the balance between good and evil.

From northern India, chess spread quickly to Persia, and after the Arabian conquest during the 600s, it reached the Arab world. Chess thrived in the Golden Age of Islam between the 700s and 1000s. The Arabs were great mathematicians, and the geometric nature of chess complemented their scientific interests.

Chess arrived in Europe by a variety of different trade routes, as well as the Moorish invasion of Spain in the 700s and the Islamic conquest of Sicily not long after. The Vikings also took the game further westward. By the beginning of the 1000s, chess was already well-known across Europe.

Chess traveled from northern India into Persia and then the Arab world. We are able to play through games recorded at that time.

The Isle of Lewis pieces are carved from walrus ivory and depict characters in a variety of bad moods—from rage to gloom.

THE EVOLVING GAME

During the later Middle Ages, between 1100 and 1450, chess established itself as the most popular board game in Europe—among the ruling classes. It was not until the 1900s that chess became a game played by millions of ordinary people.

During the long history of chess, the different pieces have inspired a wide variety of designs.

A MIRROR OF SOCIETY

The names of the pieces that we use today—the king, queen, bishop, and knight—were established during the Middle Ages, when society was very ordered and geared toward warfare. Chess reflected this rigid world, and it found a place in many ballads and poems of the period.

DYNAMIC CHANGES

After the 1450s, during the period known as the Renaissance, the rules of chess evolved into the ones with which we are familar. As society and cultural life became more dynamic, so did chess. The queen, which until then had had limited powers, now became the most powerful piece on the board. The bishop also extended its range, and pawns were permitted to move two squares at the outset. These rule changes meant that a lightning attack was possible right from the very beginning of the game.

The earliest European study of chess is a Spanish work that dates from the 1200s.

When this Italian picture of two chess-playing sisters was painted in 1555, the rules of the game had settled into the ones we know today.

CHESS ON THE MOVE

Many different cultures and places have produced great chess players over the centuries. In the Renaissance, Spain and Italy were the strongest chess-playing nations. From the middle of the 1700s, Paris produced many excellent players, and in the middle of the 1800s, London became the center of chess life. In the early 1900s, chess ceased to be a game played exclusively by the idle rich. Centers of excellence sprang up all over the world—in central and eastern Europe (Berlin, Vienna, Budapest, and Moscow), and in North and South America.

At the start of the 2000s, China and India are the emerging chess super-powers, reflecting the development of technology. Powered by the internet, chess has truly become a game played in every corner of the globe, at any time of day. There are numerous chess websites where players can play games, practice tactical skills, watch top players in battle, and engage with popular streamers on sites such as Twitch and YouTube. Chess has become one of the fastest growing esports with millions of games played every day and professional tournaments attracting major sponsors.

LIVING HISTORY

In the long and varied history of chess, each generation has built upon the experience and knowledge of the preceding one. Records about the game have survived down the ages—they let us trace a clear line of thinking that goes right back to the earliest days of the game. Whenever you play chess you are taking part in an ancient activity and making a direct link with players who lived almost 1,500 years ago.

During the 1800s, chess clubs sprang up across Europe. Matches took place in coffee houses, important social meeting places at this time.

Nowadays, more games are played online than with physical pieces.

The strongest computer programs are able to defeat the best human chess players. Professional players use them to practice ideas when training for tournaments.

SETTING UP

King Queen Rook Bishop Knight Pawn

Chess is a game played by two players on a board of 64 squares, half of them white (or a pale color) and the other half black (or dark). One player commands the white pieces, the other the black pieces, taking it in turns to move. White always makes the first move at the beginning of the game.

When positioning the board at the beginning of the game, make sure there is a white square in the right-hand corner. As well as being part of the rules, this helps you to set up the pieces for the start of the game.

The pieces are always set up in exactly the same way for the beginning of the game. On the first row of squares (or "rank") stand the most important pieces. The rooks—sometimes called castles—sit in the corners. Next to them on both sides of the board are the knights. Then come the bishops and finally, on the middle two squares, stand the king and queen.

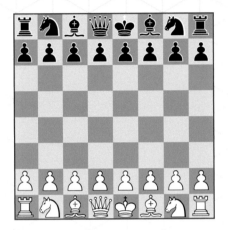

In this book the chessboard and pieces are often represented by a simple diagram. If you are not sure which piece is which, you can refer back to the diagram.

Be sure to put the king and queen on the right squares. There is an easy rule to help you do this – the queen stands on its own colour. In other words, if you have a white queen it will be placed on the white square nearest the middle. If you have a black queen it will stand on the black square nearest the middle. In front of these pieces, on the second rank, is a row of eight pawns.

Pieces should always be placed in the middle of the squares. Only one piece is allowed on a square at a time. However, enemy pieces can be captured by moving onto a square that is occupied and removing that piece.

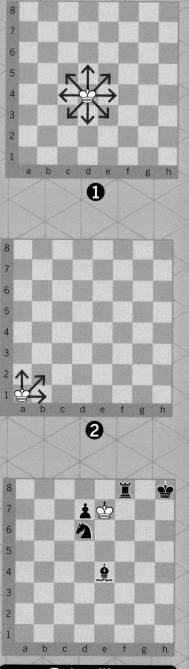

❶

❷

Test position

Which pieces can the White king take? Answer on page 60.

THE KING

The king is easy to recognize. In most chess sets it is the tallest piece and it always has a small cross on the top of its crown.

The king is the most important piece on the chessboard. The whole game revolves around the struggle to trap the king. This is called checkmate. Lose this piece and you lose the game, so it is vital that you keep the king as secure as possible. It is usually best to tuck the king away at the side of the board and surround it with a protective shield of pawns—just as political leaders in real life are protected by bodyguards. If a king loses the cover of its pieces, it is likely to fall prey to an attack by the enemy army because it cannot move out of danger very quickly.

The king is the most important piece, but it is actually one of the least powerful. It is only allowed to move one square at a time, although it may move in any direction. It can capture other pieces, but it cannot move to a square where it might be captured, or put in check. For now, just try to familiarize yourself with its basic moves (**diagrams 1 and 2**).

There is also one special move, or leap, that the king can make just once in the game. This is called castling, and it is explained on **page 24**.

DID YOU KNOW ?

Chess is sometimes known as the Royal Game. Kings and queens have played chess for centuries, including William the Conqueror, who is said to have broken a chessboard over a French prince's head.

THE ROOK

At the start of the game you have two rooks in your army of pieces. They stand at the corners of the board looking like the turrets of a castle. Some players call the piece the "castle," although the proper name is rook.

Rooks are powerful pieces, but at the beginning of the game they are unable to move at all because they are hemmed in by the other pieces. They really come into their own later on, when the game has opened up.

Rooks are able to move up and down and side to side on the board, unless there is something blocking their path. They cannot leap over other pieces, except when they perform the special move of "castling" (**see page 24**).

In this position (**diagram 1**), the rook can move to any of the squares marked by the arrows. Compare the mobility of the rook to the limited range of the king. It is like the difference between a tortoise and a hare.

The rook can zoom from one side of the board to the other, but only if there is nothing in its way. Here, for instance, it cannot move past the White king (**diagram 2**).

DID YOU KNOW ?

The word "rook" derives from an old Arabic word "rukh," meaning chariot. By the time chess reached Europe, sometime after A.D. 700, chariots were no longer in use. Instead, the rook came to resemble a castle's turret, which more accurately reflected the nature of society and warfare during the Middle Ages.

❶

❷

Test position

Which pieces can the White rook take? Answer on page 60.

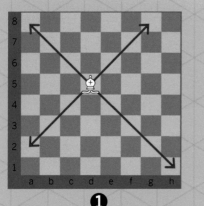

❶

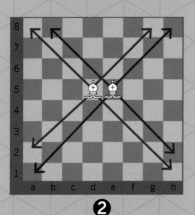

❷

Test position

Which pieces can the White bishop take? Answers on page 60.

THE BISHOP

Next to the king and queen at the start of the game you will find the bishops. This reflects their status in European medieval society, when the clergy were at the heart of government, crucial advisors to the ruling monarchs.

The bishop may move forward or backward along the diagonals for as many squares as it likes, as long as there is nothing standing in its way. The bishop can move to any of the squares along the lines of the arrows (**diagram 1**).

Both sides have two bishops, one that runs along the dark squares of the board, the other on the light squares. A bishop that begins on a white square can only move along the white squares. A bishop that begins on a black square must keep to the black squares (**diagram 2**).

A "bishop pair" can be very powerful in an open position, exerting influence right across the board. They are often best placed at the edges, far away from marauding enemy pieces, but still able to make their presence felt across the center and the opposite side of the board.

DID YOU KNOW ?

When the game of chess began in India, the bishops were known as "elephants." In many languages the name still survives to this day. In Russian, for example, the word "slon." which means elephant, is used to refer to the bishop.

THE QUEEN

The queen is easy to recognize—it always has a crown at the top of the piece, and is just a bit shorter than the king, which it stands next to at the start of the game.

The queen is able to move up and down and across the board like a rook, as well as along the diagonals like a bishop, as long as there is nothing blocking its path. When it is in the center of the board the queen exercises extraordinary power (**diagram 1**).

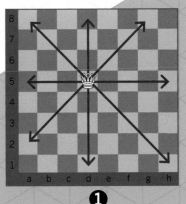

❶

The queen does not have to stand in the middle of the board in order to have a decisive impact on the game. Even from the corner, the queen's influence stretches right across to the other side of the board. The queen is able to move to any of the squares along the marked arrows (**diagram 2**).

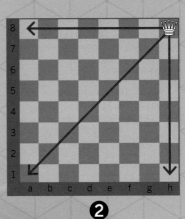

❷

Although the king is the most important piece in your army, the queen is actually the most powerful. This means that you should take good care of this piece—if the queen is lost, defeat is often inevitable. Try not to move the queen out too early in the game. First, make sure that you have found a safe square for it.

Test position

Which pieces can the White queen take? Answers on page 60.

DID YOU KNOW ?

In the original game in India and Persia, this piece—the "vizier"—actually had very limited powers. However, after the 1400s, the queen became a more powerful piece, in keeping with a changing and more dynamic society.

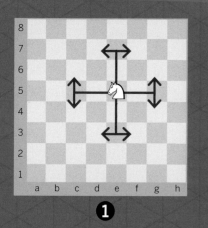

①

②

Test position

Which pieces can the Black knight take? Answers on page 60.

THE KNIGHT

The knight is one of the craftiest members of your army. It has the unique ability to leap over other pieces. This, combined with its sidestepping movement, can make it a difficult piece to deal with.

The knight moves two squares in a straight direction, and then one to the side, either to the left or the right. It might be easier if you think of the move as a kind of L-shape (**diagram 1**).

The knight makes the game more dynamic. In positions that appear blocked it can force a breakthrough because it is the only chess piece that is able to leap over other pieces. Here, for instance, it can capture the bishop that stands on the other side of the pawns (**diagram 2**).

Because the knight is a short-range piece, it often functions poorly at the side or the corner of the board, where its scope is limited. You will find that it is much more effective to keep your knights in the middle of the board where they have more options.

DID YOU KNOW ?
As far as we know, the L-shaped knight move has remained the same since the beginnings of the game in India at the end of the 6th century. This leaping piece has always been associated with the cavalry.

THE PAWN

Eight pawns stand in front of your pieces. They are the foot soldiers, the least valuable members of your army. Nevertheless, they still perform a very important role in the game.

On their first move, pawns are able to advance either two squares, or one. After this, they are only allowed to move forward one square at a time (**diagram 1**). They cannot move backward or sideways. Among other duties, pawns are used to mark out territory before the most important pieces advance into battle.

Unlike all the other pieces, pawns progress straight up theboard, but they capture one square diagonally forward. The other pieces capture in the same direction that they move. Here, for instance, White could choose to take either the rook or the knight (**diagram 2**).

Pawns have one special property that can prove decisive in many games. If a pawn reaches the other side of the board, it must immediately transform into another piece —a knight, bishop, rook, or queen (**diagram 3**). In practice, most people choose a new queen as it is the most powerful piece on the board. Promoting a pawn occurs most frequently at the end of the game when there are fewer pieces to obstruct the progress of the pawn down the board.

1

2

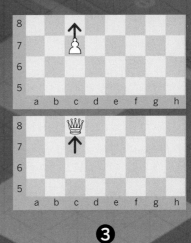

3

NOTATION

Chess games from hundreds of years ago have survived to this day because the moves were recorded. In the past, a variety of methods were used to note the moves, but it is the "algebraic system" that now predominates throughout the world.

ALGEBRAIC NOTATION

"Algebraic notation" sounds far more complicated than it actually is. If you have ever found a place on a map, then you will already be familiar with the system. Algebraic notation is based on a simple grid system of eight letters and eight numbers. By combining a letter with a number, it makes it very easy to identify each square, as the diagrams on this page show.

It is important to learn chess notation if you want to understand the many diagrams in this book, or to read other chess books and magazines. Later, you will also be able to record your games for posterity!

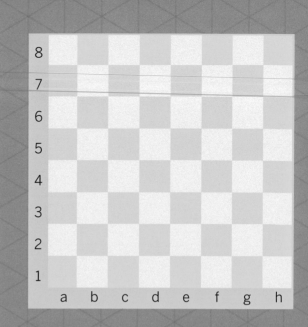

The rows of squares going up the board, the files, are each given a letter, from a to h. The rows of squares across the board are known as ranks. These are given a number from 1 to 8. Using this system, it is easy to identify each square on the chessboard with a letter and a number.

8	a8	b8	c8	d8	e8	f8	g8	h8
7	a7	b7	c7	d7	e7	f7	g7	h7
6	a6	b6	c6	d6	e6	f6	g6	h6
5	a5	b5	c5	d5	e5	f5	g5	h5
4	a4	b4	c4	d4	e4	f4	g4	h4
3	a3	b3	c3	d3	e3	f3	g3	h3
2	a2	b2	c2	d2	e2	f2	g2	h2
1	a1	b1	c1	d1	e1	f1	g1	h1
	a	b	c	d	e	f	g	h

For example, the square in the bottom right-hand corner is known as h1—the letter is always put before the number. No matter which side of the board you sit at, the numbers and letters remain the same. The h1 square is always in White's bottom right-hand corner.

Apart from the pawn, each piece is identified by a single capital letter:

K King
Q Queen
R Rook
B Bishop
N Knight

To avoid confusion with the king, the knight is given the phonetic N. The pieces are always identified with capital letters. For the squares, lower case letters are used.

1 Take a look at this position. The rook moves up the board and Black responds by moving a pawn. These moves would be recorded in the following way: **1 Rd7 c6**.

2 The **1** is the move number, the **R** stands for the rook, **d7** identifies the square the rook moves to. Black's move is given in the second column. The pawn moves to the **c6** square. Pawns are not identified by a letter—only the square they move to is recorded.

Here is a simple test. Set your pieces up for the start of the game and play out the following moves on your board (the x indicates a capture and the + means check).

1 e4 c5
2 Nf3 d6
3 d4 cxd4
4 Nxd4 Nf6
5 Bb5+ Nbd7

You should have reached the position in **diagram 3**.

3 On the third move, notice that when Black's pawn captures, the file it comes from is noted (an exception to the rule that only the destination of the piece is recorded). In this case the pawn was on the c-file, and it captured a piece on the d4 square, so it is written **3...cxd4**. (The three dots are a standard convention to indicate that this is Black's move, not White's). On the fifth move, both of Black's knights could move to the d7 square, therefore a b is used to indicate which one goes there, in this case the knight standing on the b-file.

CHECK AND CHECKMATE 1

Now that you know how the pieces move, it is time to tackle the principles of check and checkmate.

Checkmating your opponent's king is the ultimate aim in a chess game. The term comes from the ancient Persian "shah mat," meaning "the king is defeated." You have to threaten the enemy king with one of your pieces so that it is unable to move and escape capture. A checkmate usually occurs when one side's forces—or "army"—are overwhelmingly superior, or by a direct and unexpected assault on the king.

DID YOU KNOW ?
Many players like to announce "check," but under the rules of the game it is not necessary to do so. Often, a player says it just to rattle their opponent. Chess can be a dirty business!

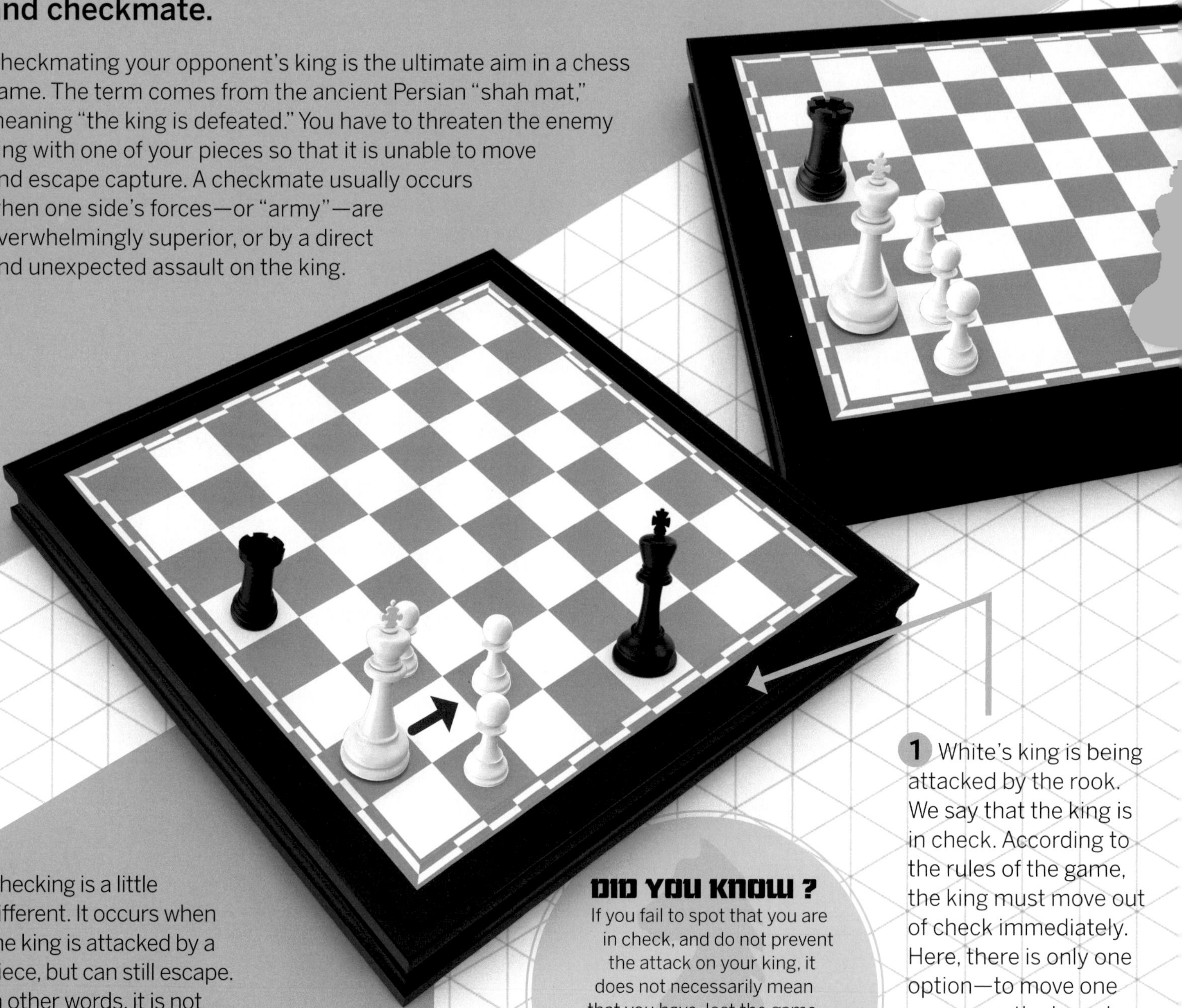

Checking is a little different. It occurs when the king is attacked by a piece, but can still escape. In other words, it is not necessarily fatal. The positions illustrated above demonstrate what the terms mean.

DID YOU KNOW ?
If you fail to spot that you are in check, and do not prevent the attack on your king, it does not necessarily mean that you have lost the game. Your opponent has to let you take your move back. You must then play another move that gets you out of the check.

1 White's king is being attacked by the rook. We say that the king is in check. According to the rules of the game, the king must move out of check immediately. Here, there is only one option—to move one square up the board.

2 This time, the position has changed a little. White's king is again in check from the rook, but now there is no escape. The king is trapped by its own pieces and cannot move out of check, so we say it is checkmated. The game is over and White has lost!

WHAT IS THE ADVANTAGE OF CHECKING?

Don't panic if your opponent suddenly thumps down a piece and cries "check." It does not end the game, and it does not always benefit your opponent. So what exactly is the point of checking?

• A check can help you gain time.

• Checking can drive the enemy king to a weak square, making it vulnerable to further attack.

TEST POSITIONS

To make sure you understand the concepts of check and checkmate, here are six test positions for you to solve. You have to figure out if it is check or checkmate, and if it is only check, how do you escape? The solutions are on the next two pages.

1 (Black to play)
Is this check or checkmate?

2 (Black to play)
Is this check or checkmate?

3 (White to play)
Is this check or checkmate?

4 (Black to play)
Is this check or checkmate?

5 (White to play)
Is this check or checkmate?

6 (White to play)
Is this check or checkmate?

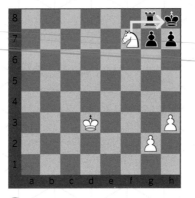

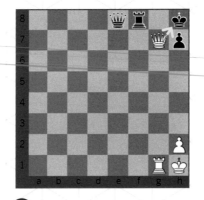

1 In this position, Black has been checkmated. White's knight is directly attacking the king, but the king is unable to escape because it is smothered by its own pieces.

2 Black has been checkmated here, too. The king is trapped in the corner and is in check from White's queen. It cannot take the queen, which is protected by the rook standing on g1.

3 White has been checkmated. The king is in check from the rook, and cannot escape. It cannot move to b3 or b1 —the knight has both squares covered.

CHECK AND CHECKMATE II —ANSWERS

4 Black's king is in check from the bishop, but it is not checkmate. The Black king can get out of danger by moving one square to the side.

5 White is in check but it is not checkmate. It is possible to advance the pawn on g2 one square to block the queen's check. Black would then be ill-advised to take the pawn on g3 with the queen—it is protected by the pawn on h2.

6 Black's queen is checking White's king in the corner of the board. However, it is not checkmate because White's rook can take Black's queen, leaving White with an overwhelming advantage.

The last three positions demonstrate the three methods of getting out of check— move the king away, block the check, or capture the piece that is checking.

When you are thinking about how to get out of check, remember these three key words: Away, Block, or Capture—ABC.

MATERIAL CHESS

Checkmating your opponent is the ultimate aim in a game of chess. But what is the best strategy to achieve this goal?

You will often find that your opponent's king is surrounded by a wall of pieces. When this happens a direct attack might not succeed. This is when a more effective strategy known as "material chess" comes into play.

In most cases, for a checkmating attack to succeed, you need to have a superiority of forces. So, at first, your strategy should be to protect your own army. At the same time you should also be thinking of ways to trap and take your opponent's pieces. It is not advisable to go after the enemy king until you have a greater number of pieces than your opponent. So before each move, you need to ask yourself two important questions:
1) Can I capture any enemy pieces?
2) Are any of my pieces threatened?

Take a look at the following positions, keeping the above questions in mind.

1 Imagine that you are White. Is Black threatening to take any of your pieces? Can you capture any of Black's?

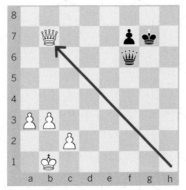

2 There are no threats from Black, so White is free to send the queen to the other side of the board and capture Black's knight.

3 Imagine you are Black. Are any of your pieces under attack? Can you capture any of White's pieces?

4 None of Black's pieces are threatened so you are free to make an attack. There is a pawn on the b4 square which the bishop can snatch: **1...Bxb4**. Black has won a pawn.

5 You might have noticed that Black can make another capture in diagram 3. The queen can take White's bishop on e3. Isn't it better to grab a bishop rather than a pawn?

6 Not in this case. White would then be able to capture the queen, winning a decisive advantage in pieces.

The last example (**diagram 6**) leads us to an important aspect of chess—how much each piece is actually worth. The value of each piece is based on its power on the board. Remembering these values will help you decide which pieces to exchange, and which pieces to keep.

The queen, with its ability to move like a rook and a bishop, is by far the most powerful piece on the board. It therefore has the highest value: 9 points. Next comes the rook with 5 points. The bishop and the knight are both worth 3 points, and finally comes the lowly pawn, with just one point. Remember that these are just rough values. In some positions a bishop is far more effective than a knight—and vice versa. Even so, they provide a useful guide when we are trying to make a tricky decision in the heat of the battle.

For example, in the last diagram, it would make no sense to capture the bishop with the queen. White would gain a queen worth nine points, and only lose a bishop worth just three points. A good rate of exchange for White—but not for Black!

You will often win a game by first capturing more pieces than your opponent. You can then wear your enemy down to an endgame. At this stage of the game you are more likely to be in a position to promote a pawn into a new queen and only then launch an attack on the king.

But remember, chess games are not won just by gathering enemy pieces. Don't lose sight of the ultimate goal—checkmate!

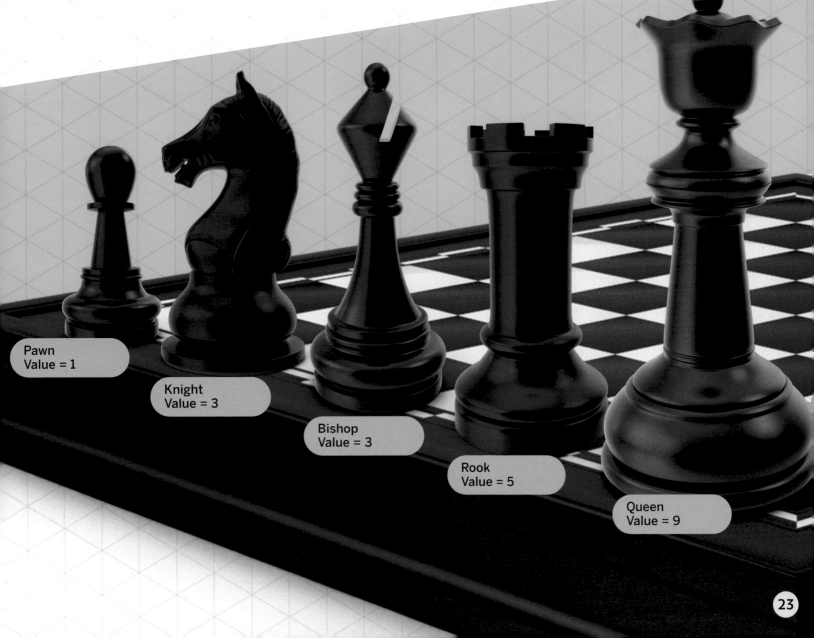

Pawn
Value = 1

Knight
Value = 3

Bishop
Value = 3

Rook
Value = 5

Queen
Value = 9

SPECIAL MOVES

There is one special move during a game when both the king and the rook can leave their starting squares on the same turn. This move is called castling. It can be a highly effective way of protecting your king.

Castling brings the king, your most important piece, to a safe place at the side of the board. It also enables one of your most powerful pieces, the rook, to enter the game. All this with just one move!

You can castle on both sides of the board. Kingside castling (**diagram 1 and 2**) is also known as "short castling." Queenside castling (**diagrams 3 and 4**) is called "long castling'" because there are more squares between the king and the rook on this side of the board.

1 The king moves two squares to the right along the first rank, and the rook leaps over and lands on the square next to it.

2 After castling, the king is at the side of the board. This is a much safer position than in the middle.

3 It is also possible to castle on the other side of the board. Once again, the king moves two squares along the first rank, this time to the left, and the rook leaps over and next to the king on the other side.

4 This is known as queenside castling or long castling. Notice that the king is not as deep in the corner as it is in kingside castling.

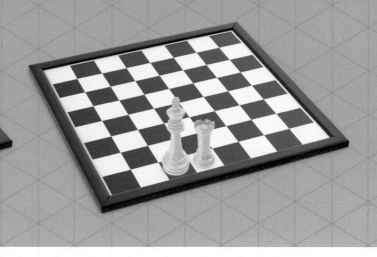

THE RULES OF CASTLING

Castling might appear a little tricky at first, but try to familiarize yourself with the rules as quickly as possible, as this is such a vital move.

- You cannot castle if your king has already moved.

- You cannot castle if your rook has already moved.

- You cannot castle if your king is in check on that turn.

- You cannot castle if your king lands into a check.

- Your king cannot castle through the line of another piece.

- You cannot castle if there is a piece standing in the way of the king or rook.

Here is an example of castling (**diagrams 5 and 6**) that should help make things clear.

EN PASSANT

It's not only the rook and king that can make a special move. There is also an unusual kind of pawn capture, which is only available in a particular situation (**see diagrams 7 and 8**). The rule, which is known as "en passant," is a legacy from five hundred years ago when pawns were first allowed to advance two squares on their opening move.

The "en passant" capture is available only when a pawn advances two squares from its starting position on a file adjacent to an enemy pawn on the fifth rank.

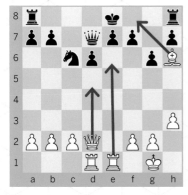

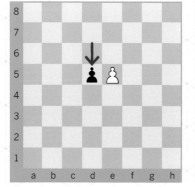

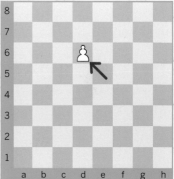

5 Black's king is under severe pressure from White's rooks and queen in the middle of the board. It's time to evacuate the king from the center. Black cannot castle on the kingside—the king is not allowed to move through the line of the bishop, which covers the f8 square. However, it is possible to castle on the queenside.

6 A great side-step by Black's king. Castling has enabled the king to move closer to the security of the corner of the board, and Black's rook, which was languishing at the side, enters the fray.

7 If a pawn moves out two squares from its starting position, then an enemy pawn standing next to it on the fifth rank is able to capture it.

8 The White pawn moves one square diagonally behind the Black pawn, and removes it from the board. It's as if the Black pawn had only moved one square.

If a player is to capture "en passant," it must be done on the turn immediately after the opposition pawn has moved two squares, or the option disappears.

OPENING THE GAME

Now that you have mastered the basic principles of chess, you are ready to learn about the most effective ways of getting a game under way. This initial phase of the game is known as the opening.

At the beginning of the game most of your pieces are boxed in. Only the pawns, which stand in front of the other pieces, can move along with the knights, which are able to leap over the pawns to the third rank.

Here are the first few moves of a game where White does all the right things, and Black makes plenty of mistakes. But we can learn from those errors, too!

① **1 e4 e5** Moving the pawn two squares to e4 is one of the best opening moves. The pawn not only controls crucial squares in the middle of the board, but it frees the way for the queen and bishop to enter the game. Black replies in the same way. **2 d4.**

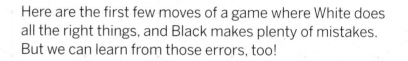

② A bold central advance by White, putting pressure on Black's center and allowing the other bishop to enter the game. **2...exd4 3 c3**

③ Understandably, Black has captured the pawn in the middle of the board, and White replies by offering another! Was that wise? **3...dxc3 4 Nxc3**

④ Black grabs the second pawn and White recaptures with the knight. White is playing a "gambit." This is when a piece is given up in the opening in order to free up your other pieces. **4...Nc6 5 Bc4 Nf6 6 Nf3**

5 White has brought out a bishop and a knight, and Black has brought out two knights. These are all strong moves because they help to control important squares in the center of the board. **6...Qe7 7 0-0** (This is how kingside castling is recorded.)

6 Black's last move was dubious. The queen is in danger of being attacked by less valuable pieces, so for the moment it should not be moved. White's last move was excellent. Castling brings the king to the side of the board where it is protected by a row of pawns, and also brings the rook into play. **7...Nxe4**

7 Black falls for a trap! Another pawn is taken, but this opens the center leaving the king in great danger. **8 Nxe4 Qxe4 9 Re1**

8 A total disaster for Black. The queen is attacked by the rook but is unable to move away as the king would then be in check. In other words, the queen will be lost. We say that the queen is "pinned" to the king (there is more on the tactic of "pinning" on **pages 28-29**).

White did well, but Black's play was poor. There are three opening principles that should be kept in mind when playing the first few moves of the game:

1) Control the center
If you control the center of the board, then you control the game. You will also find it easier to deal with any difficulties as the game develops.

2) Bring out your pieces
On the chessboard it is vital that your entire army comes into play as quickly as possible. If your pieces are too slow, the battle could be lost before you know it.

3) Castle
Remember, your king is the most important piece but, at the same time, one of the least powerful. By castling as quickly as possible, it can be put in a safe position. You will also find that bringing the rook from the corner into play can be very useful in the fight for the center.

DANGER!!
Do not move your queen out too early in the game. It is liable to be attacked and driven back by weaker pieces. Although the queen is your most powerful piece, it still needs the support of the rest of your army.

FORKS, PINS, AND SKEWERS,

Forks, pins and skewers are some of the sneakiest tricks you can use against your opponent. These tactics can lead to winning one, and sometimes several, enemy pieces, and, ultimately, this can lead to winning the game.

Although it is unlikely that you will find the positions on the opposite page duplicated exactly in your own games, you will soon begin to recognize similar positions. The more you play, the more familiar you will become with these highly effective and often deadly ruses.

THE FORK

This is a simultaneous attack on two enemy pieces. The most common fork is made by the knight (**diagram 1**). Knight forks feature in many games, so it is important to familiarize yourself with the move—for your own safety! Pawns can also make effective two-pronged attacks (**diagram 2**). The bishop and the knight are frequently the target of pawn forks.

THE PIN

The pin is an attack against two enemy pieces standing on the same line. Like the fork, this is also extremely common. We have already encountered a pin on page 27 (**diagram 8**). On that occasion, a rook pinned the queen to the king. This time (**diagrams 3 and 4**) the pin is a little different.

THE SKEWER

This can be a deadly maneuvre. The skewer attack operates by piercing through one piece to trap another standing on the same rank, file, or diagonal. The second piece is the real target (**diagrams 5 and 6**).

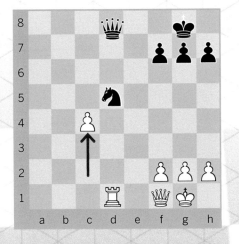

1 White's knight has leaped in, checking Black's king, and at the same time attacking the queen. Lethal! Black must move the king out of check, then the knight captures the queen on the next turn.

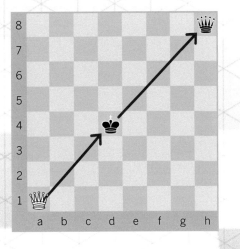

2 This is another example of a fork, this time by a pawn. Black's pawn has just advanced, simultaneously attacking the bishop and the knight. One of the pieces can be saved, but not both, so Black wins material. (Remember, a pawn is worth just one point and the bishop and knight three.)

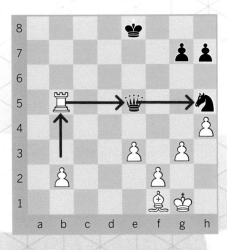

3 Here is a very effective pin. Black's bishop has moved out to attack the queen. White's queen cannot escape as the king would then be in check. The best that White can do is to take the bishop with the queen —but then lose this key piece to the Black knight on the following move.

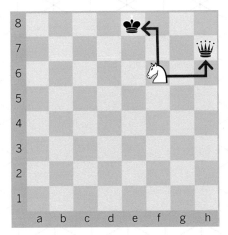

4 In this position, White's pawn moves up to attack the knight in a classic case of how to exploit a pin. If Black's knight moves, then the queen will be taken by the rook. There is no escape—the capture of Black's knight has become inevitable.

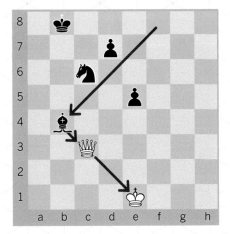

5 A skewer can be a deadly piece of play. Here, Black's king is in check from White's queen. The king must move out of check. White's queen will then capture Black's queen.

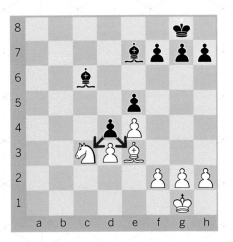

6 White's rook has just moved to b5, attacking the queen. The queen must move as it is Black's most valuable piece. But, when it does, White's rook can capture the exposed knight.

FOUR LETHAL ATTACKS

There are many cunning and devious ways to make an attack. Some occur with such frequency that they have been given specific names—as we have just seen. Here are a few more lethal weapons to add to your armory.

DISCOVERED CHECK

Although it has a slightly confusing name (like a lot of chess jargon) this can be very effective. Discovered check is when one piece is moved allowing another piece to give check (**diagrams 1 and 2**).

DIAGONAL BATTERY

You might think that a castled king position is quite safe. After all, it is at the side of the board, away from the exposed center, and, in this case (**diagram 3**), protected by pawns. But a castled king is not invulnerable.

1 Look at the position of Black's rook in relation to White's king. It would be check if it weren't for Black's knight which sits in between the two. That gives Black an idea. The knight could be moved out of the way, putting White's king in check from the rook. Now comes the clever bit. Why not move the knight so that it attacks the queen?

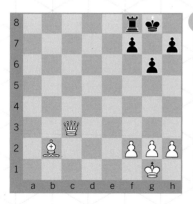

3 White has craftily lined up a battery of fire-power—the queen is in front of the bishop on the so-called "long diagonal." In this position the White queen can inflict maximum damage.

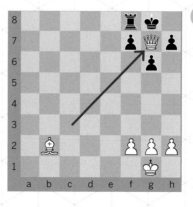

4 Black's king cannot get out of check—the White queen is covered by the bishop. Checkmate! Here it was very easy for White to set up the battery of queen and bishop but, in the cut and thrust of battle, it may not be so simple. Even so, watch out for this deadly attack in your games.

SEVENTH HEAVEN

At the start of a game, the rooks, trapped in the corners, struggle to make their mark on the game. However, later on, when pieces have been cleared from the board, the rooks play a more prominent role, zooming down open files. If they are able to reach the seventh rank, they can be extremely dangerous, capturing pawns and pinning the enemy king to the side of the board (**diagrams 5 and 6**).

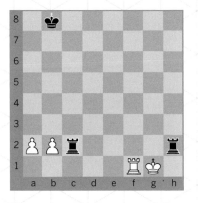

5 The two Black rooks have both made it to the seventh rank. Nothing can stop them from sweeping up everything in their path. Now they even have the chance to deliver the final blow.

6 The rook sweeps over to deliver checkmate to the helpless king—it cannot capture the rook which is now supported by its comrade. Two rooks on the seventh rank are exceptionally powerful but even a single rook should not be underestimated.

BACK RANK MATE

We now move one rank further down, from the seventh to the eighth, the last or "back" rank. We already know that the sooner one castles in a game, the better. However, as we've seen, even after castling you must still take care.

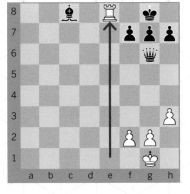

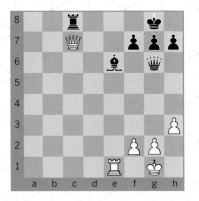

2 Brilliant!
The knight has moved out of the way of the rook, putting White's king in check. The king must get out of check, then on the next turn Black's knight takes the queen, the most powerful piece on the board. This will leave Black with a rook and a knight against a lone king—more than enough pieces to force a checkmate.

7 Black's rook has just moved to c8, threatening to capture the queen. At first glance, the move appears safe as the bishop covers the rook. But White has spotted that the back rank is vulnerable and sacrifices the queen: **1 Qxc8+**. Black must recapture with the bishop: **1 ...Bxc8**. Then the rook rockets to the eighth rank: **2 Re8**.

8 It's checkmate. Black's king is unable to escape from the rook's check—it is blocked in by its own pawns. Checkmate could have been avoided by pushing out one of the pawns in front of the castled king (as White has done in this position) so that the king has an escape route if there is ever a check on the eighth rank.

SACRIFICE!

In chess, a sacrifice is when a piece is given up for greater gain. For instance, it might result in winning enemy pieces or, in the best case, even forcing a checkmate.

The word "sacrifice" has associations with ancient religion—animals were once sacrificed on the altar to appease a god. You should keep in mind why a sacrifice is made—for the greater good of the community, in this case, your army of chess pieces, and the ultimate goal of checkmate. A sacrifice can come as a great surprise to your opponent. Just as in a real battle, surprise is one of the most useful weapons at your disposal.

Making a sacrifice is thrilling but it is also risky. For instance, you might miscalculate, so that when the smoke clears, the balance is negative—you are left with fewer pieces than your opponent. It is important, therefore, to weigh up the options carefully before committing yourself.

1 White has two rooks storming down a file, but so far Black's defences are holding firm. But now comes the knock-out punch. **1 Qxh7+** Shocking! White sacrifices the queen for just one pawn. Black has no alternative but to capture: **1...Kxh7**.

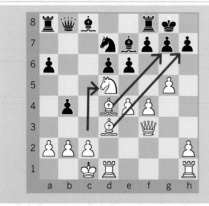

DID YOU KNOW ?

In the history of chess, arguably the greatest exponent of the sacrifice was the Latvian, Mikhail Tal (1936–1992). He was able to conjure up an attack from nowhere by playing the most unexpected sacrifices. Here Tal (White) throws a knight into the middle of the board, inviting his opponent to capture it with the pawn. He realized that in return for the piece, the full force of the bishops would be unleashed on Black's king. In the end, Tal's opponent was unable to resist the pressure of the attack and lost the game.

2 And now we see the point. Black's king has been brought out into the open so that White is now able to play: **2 Rh4.** Checkmate. Superb. White's rook checks the king which has no escape—the other rook covers the only flight square. It is no consolation that at the end of the game Black is a queen up.

Not all sacrifices are as dramatic as this first example. Often they are played just to win some enemy pieces. **Diagrams 3 and 4** show a typical case in which White gives up a rook (worth 5 points) for a bishop (worth only 3) but the investment is repaid.

3 White, with two extra pawns, is already doing well, but the easiest way to finish the game is to play **1 Rxf8+**. Black's king then takes the rook **1...Kxf8**. The point of the sacrifice is to set up a knight fork—Black's king has been forced to the perfect square: **2 Nd7+**. Black's king must now move out of check.

4 **2...Ke7 3 Nxb8**. The knight captures the rook on b8, leaving White in a winning position. One of the pawns can eventually be forced to the eighth rank, making a new queen.

Let's check the balance at the end of this skirmish. White gave up a rook (worth 5 points), but gained a rook and a bishop (worth 5 and 3 points). White came out on top.

WHAT IS A DRAW?

When you play a game of chess, winning and losing are not the only possible outcomes. If neither side is able to force a checkmate, then the game is a draw. In serious tournament play, about half of all games end this way.

Just because a game is drawn, it does not mean that it has not been hard-fought; it is inevitable that sometimes an immovable force meets an irresistible object! There are a number of ways in which a game may end in a draw.

INSUFFICIENT MATING MATERIAL

If neither side has enough pieces left at the end of the game, then the position is declared drawn (**see diagram 1**).

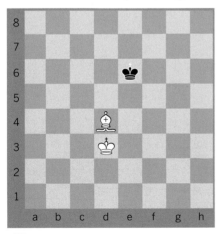

1 For instance, here, the game is drawn because it is impossible to checkmate with just a lone bishop—you can try if you like, but you won't get anywhere! Likewise, king and knight against a king is a draw. A pawn is less powerful than a knight, so you might assume that king and pawn against king is also a draw —but this is not always the case. Sometimes it is possible to force the pawn to the eighth rank to get a new queen, and it is possible to checkmate with a king and queen. It is also possible to checkmate with a king and rook.

2 Black, with three extra pawns, is hoping for a win. However, White can force a draw. Black's king is in check from the queen, so it must move. The king moves back one square: **1...Kg8**. White continues pursuing the king: **2 Qd8+**.

3 Black's king is in check again, so it must move up the board, once more maintaining protection of the queen: **2...Kg7**. Now White can repeat the position we started with by playing the queen back, giving another check: **3 Qd4+**. This is the second repetition of the position. White repeats again: **3...Kg8 4 Qd8+ Kg7**. Now White can claim a draw because the position can be repeated for a third time with the following move: **5 Qd4+**. A lucky escape.

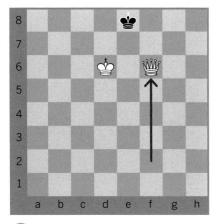

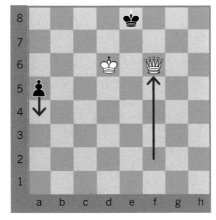

4 With an extra queen against a lone king, White is hoping for a swift checkmate. White closes in with the queen for the kill, but comes a little too close. Black's king has no legal moves. However, this does not mean that Black is checkmated. The king is not in check—this is the crucial difference. This position is "stalemate" and is a draw.

5 This is the same position as the last one, with the crucial difference that Black has one remaining pawn. Again, White's queen closes in, and this time it is strong. Although Black's king cannot move, the position is NOT stalemate. Black still has one legal move: **1...a4**, then White's queen delivers checkmate: **2 Qe7**.

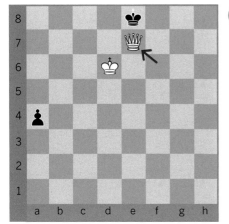

6 As you can see from this position, a single pawn can make all the difference between winning and drawing.

REPETITION OF POSITION

If the same position occurs three times in a game, then the player whose move it is can claim a draw (**diagrams 2 and 3**).

STALEMATE

Stalemate is something to watch out for when one side has an overwhelming superiority in forces, and is moving in for a checkmate against an exposed king. Stalemate is when a player cannot make any legal moves but is not in check (**diagrams 4, 5, and 6**).

THE FIFTY-MOVE RULE

This is an extremely rare way of making a draw. If a piece is not captured and a pawn is not moved for 50 moves, then the game may be declared drawn. This is a very rare occurrence—games of chess are not usually so boring!

AGREEING ON A DRAW

The most common way to make a draw in serious tournament games is simply by agreement. After making a move, a player announces: "I offer a draw." This can either be accepted or declined. However, all too often draws are offered and accepted as a way of playing it safe. It is better not to get into the habit of offering draws—cutting the game short unnaturally does nothing for your chess development.

TRAINING EXERCISES

In every serious sport you need to train regularly if you want to improve your game. Chess is no exception. Just like boxers training for an important fight, the strongest chess players in the world will spend months in preparation for a World Championship final, studying their opponent's style and strategy, and working on their own game.

WORKING OUT

There are simple exercises you can practice that will be of enormous benefit. You can either find a friend to play against or you can use chess software and spar against a machine—that is more testing!

It is extremely important to learn how to finish off your opponent at the end of the game— the techniques explained here will help you feel confident about winning.

Even when you are practicing these training exercises, try not to take any of your moves back. The following three-step plan will help you sharpen your chess mind.

1) Eyes 2) Brain 3) Hand

1) Look at the position carefully, paying particular attention to your opponent's last move.
2) Then work out what you think is the correct move.
3) Only when you are absolutely sure of your move should you reach for a piece.

First of all, have a go at checkmating with a queen and rook against a lone king (**diagram 1**). After you have tried this, take a look at the method explained below.

1 **1 Ra4**. An important first move. Instead of checking, the rook restricts the king, preventing it from moving into one half of the board. Only then it will be driven back by the queen. **1...Kf5 2 Qd5+ Kf6 3 Ra6+ Ke7 4 Qb7+ Ke8 5 Ra8**. You should have arrived at the following position (**diagram 2**).

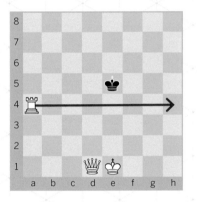

2 Black's king is in check from the rook. It is unable to escape as the queen covers all the squares on the seventh rank. Therefore, the position is checkmate. If you have practiced this mate and feel you have mastered it, try the same thing but with two rooks against a king. Use the same technique but you need to be a little more careful.

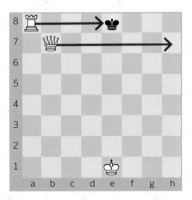

When there are just a few pieces on the board, the king becomes a powerful piece—in stark contrast to its role early on in the game when it should be hidden away as quickly as possible. The next training exercise aims to develop your skill in handling the king.

Your next exercise is a little harder than the first. You have to force checkmate using your king and queen against a lone king. It is White to play.

TIP: It is impossible for a queen to deliver checkmate on its own. It needs the assistance of the king.

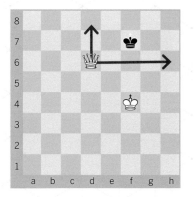

3 **1 Qd4+**. It is only possible to checkmate the king at the side of the board, so first it must be driven there. The queen gives a check, forcing the king backward. **1...Ke6 2 Kf4 Kf7 3 Qd6**.

4 Instead of checking the Black king (which in this case would only allow it to escape up the board), the queen restricts its movement. Black's king cannot escape across the force-field created by White's queen. **3...Kg7 4 Kf5**. With Black's king trapped it is time to bring up the henchman to assist in the finish. **4...Kf7 5 Qd7+ Kf8 6 Kg6 Kg8 7 Qg7**

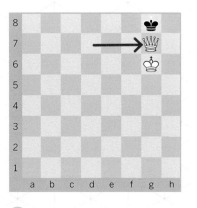

5 Black's king is in check from the queen, and there are no escape squares. The queen cannot be captured as White's king supports it. (Remember that the kings cannot stand on adjacent squares.) Therefore it's checkmate. The final position clearly shows how the attacking side must use the king to force checkmate.

6 Both sides have just a king and four pawns each. Your play needs to be subtle and highly skilled if you are going to win. You need to capture an enemy pawn with the king, then force one of your own pawns to the eighth rank to get a new queen. Then you can force a checkmate—using the techniques above.

If you feel like increasing the complexity of the position, add a few more pawns to each side. This exercise is a great way of learning how the king and pawns interact.

TEST POSITIONS

To find out how much you have learned from the first half of the book, try solving these ten test positions. You will find some easy, but others require a little bit more concentration. Try to work out the answers in your head by just studying the diagrams on these pages. If you have problems visualizing the line of play, you can always set up the positions on your chessboard. Solving chess puzzles like these is an excellent way of sharpening your skills. You will find the answers on pages 60–61.

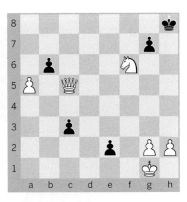

1 Of all the possible pawn moves Black could make in this position, which is the best?

2 Black can make many different captures in this position. Which one is the best?

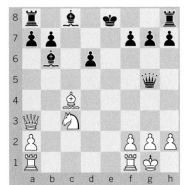

3 White is ready to launch a violent assault with moves such as **Re1+ or Qxd6**. How can Black best counter White's threat?

4 White's rook is in a great position on the seventh rank. How can this be used to gain a winning material advantage?

5 It's White's turn to play. How does White get a winning advantage from this position?

6 What should Black play here?

7 White can gain a winning advantage with the next move. Can you see how?

8 Black has just moved a pawn forward, attacking White's knight. How would you respond?

9 How does White gain a winning material advantage from this position?

10 White is four pawns down—can the situation still be saved?

THE WORLD CHAMPIONSHIP I

Every great chess player dreams of becoming the World Chess Champion. The winner of the fiercely fought World Championship joins an illustrious list of previous titleholders that goes back over a century.

CONTESTED BEGINNINGS

In 1866, a self-confident Austrian named Wilhelm Steinitz beat the German player Adolf Anderssen in a challenge match in London and duly proclaimed himself "World Chess Champion." There had never been an official World Champion before, and it was far from clear whether Steinitz should be the first.

Then in 1883, Johannes Zukertort, a Polish master who had won a few tournaments in Europe, pulled a similar trick, and also claimed to be "World Champion." Steinitz took offense, and a match was arranged in the United States, in 1886, with the title going to the first player to win ten games. The offical World Championship was born.

THE HIGHEST HONOR

Steinitz won the match, and since then there has been a clear line of successors to the title. World Champions are accorded a huge amount of respect in the chess world. There can be gaps of many years between World Championship matches, so when they take place they generate a great deal of excitement. The matches can take weeks and sometimes months to complete. and the preparation time even longer. It takes long months of physical training, mental focus, and hours of practice.

WORLD CHAMPIONS 1886-PRESENT

1886–1894 Wilhelm Steinitz introduced a new positional style to the game. This Austrian player realized it was not necessary to go for an all-out attack on the king in order to win.

1894–1921 Emanuel Lasker held the title for a record 27 years. The German was a psychologist at the chessboard, outwitting his opponents with surprising and even dubious moves. Away from chess, he was an eminent university mathematician.

1921–1927 José-Raoul Capablanca was a Cuban diplomat. He favored clear, simple positions and there was an effortless quality to his victories.

1927–1935, 1937–1946 Alexander Alekhine fled the Soviet Union in 1921. He studied chess obsessively for many hours a day. An explosive, dynamic player, he died penniless, although still in possession of his title.

1935–1937 Max Euwe a Dutch mathematician, won his first tournament aged ten. A highly logical player, he held the title for only two years.

1948–1957, 1958–1960, 1961–1963 Mikhail Botvinnik has been called the "Patriarch of Soviet Chess." He was a scientist by training and his study of all phases of the game, including the opening, was always painstakingly detailed.

1957–1958 Vassily Smyslov was born in Moscow. He was not only a brilliant chess player but also a talented musician. In his personality and style at the chessboard, he always emphasised the role of "harmony."

1960–1961 Mikhail Tal became World Champion at the age of 23 with a style of chess that was flashy and fearless. His clashes with fellow Soviet player Botvinnik proved highly memorable.

1963–1969 Tigran Petrosian was born in Armenia, in the former Soviet Union. His style of play was defensive and he was extremely hard to beat.

1969–1972 Boris Spassky was born in Russia. He loved to attack, sometimes sacrificing pieces to get to his opponent's king. However, he could never match the dedication of his great rival, Bobby Fischer.

1972–1975 Bobby Fischer was the youngest winner ever of the U.S. national championship at the age of 14. After he won the world title he dropped out of competitive chess and became a virtual recluse.

1975–1985 Anatoly Karpov learned to play chess when he was four and studied with Botvinnik. He was often compared to a python, eliminating all counterplay and gradually squeezing his opponent into submission.

1985–2000 Garry Kasparov was born in Azerbaijan and became the youngest World Champion ever at the age of 22. He has now retired from chess to pursue a career in business and politics.

2000–2007 Vladimir Kramnik is a former pupil of Kasparov. Known as "Iceberg" for his coolness under pressure, he makes his pieces work together in perfect harmony.

2007–2013 Viswanathan Anand is the first ever world champion from India. At his best, he was a frighteningly fluent player, rattling opponents with the speed of his moves.

2013–2023 Magnus Carlsen became, at the age of 19, the youngest ever player to reach the top of the world rankings. In 2022 he declared that he would not be competing in the next world championship match.

2023 Ding Liren from China became World Champion after defeating the Russian Ian Nepomniachtchi in a nerve-jangling match.

THE WORLD CHAMPIONSHIP II

When a World Championship match is played, millions of chess enthusiasts follow the games. Knowing that so many people are watching can inspire the players to perform brilliantly—or to collapse completely.

2 This leaves White with an extra knight and a pawn—at this level more than enough material advantage to force a win.

1 Petrosian (White) gives away his queen: **30 Qh8+**. A neat temporary sacrifice to drag Black's king onto a poor square. Spassky resigns immediately—a deadly knight fork occurs after **30...Kxh8 31 Nxf7+**. Black's king must get out of check: **31...Kg7** but then the knight takes the queen: **32 Nxg5.**

THE BEST MOVE IN A WORLD CHAMPIONSHIP?

The standard of play in World Championship matches has been, as one would expect, incredibly high, so it is difficult to select one spectacular play. However, this is one particularly memorable move (**diagram 1**) from the 1966 match between Tigran Petrosian and Boris Spassky. Petrosian finishes off his opponent in style.

THE WORST MOVE IN A WORLD CHAMPIONSHIP?

Besides the many great moves, there have also been a number of outright blunders. Under pressure, even the best players in the world can play some appalling moves. This miscalculation **(diagram 3)** is from the bitter world title fight in 1978 between Viktor Korchnoi, the challenger and Soviet defector, and his archenemy, Anatoly Karpov.

3 Although Karpov (Black) threatens a back-rank mate with his rook, this can be prevented quite easily by moving the g-pawn, providing an escape square for the king. Instead, Korchnoi blunders. He plays **39 Ra1**, which allows a smart finish: **39...Nf3+**, and Korchnoi resigns the game immediately. Otherwise: **40 gxf3,** then **40...Rg6+ 41 Kh1 Nf2.**

4 White's king is trapped in the corner. Checkmate.

CLASSICAL, RAPID, AND BLITZ CHAMPIONSHIPS

Traditional World Championship matches are played at a leisurely pace. The title of World Champion is the ultimate prize in chess and the players need time to think. In Classical Chess, contestants must play 40 moves in two hours, and the game continues at a similar tempo after that. Games can sometimes last as long as seven or eight hours.

However, to capture the interest of a wider audience, new events with much faster time limits have been introduced. In the World Rapid Chess Championship, the players are given just 15 minutes each at the start of the game, plus 10 seconds for every move made. If one of the players oversteps the time limit, they automatically lose, no matter what is happening on the board. As time runs out, the players have to move quickly, relying just on instinct. That is when the blunders and brilliancies occur.

The World Blitz Chess Championship is even faster. The players are given just 3 minutes at the start of the game, plus 2 seconds for every move made. The standard of play is even more varied than in Rapid Chess and the randomness adds to the fun for spectators.

Magnus Carlsen is acknowledged as the strongest chess player in the world, but even he does not always triumph in these events. In 2021 the World Rapid Chess Champion was 17-year-old Nodirbek Abdusattorov from Uzbekistan, and the World Blitz Chess Champion was Maxime Vachier-Lagrave from France, who specializes in quick games.

KING MAGNUS

For more than a decade, Magnus Carlsen has dominated the world of chess. He became World Champion in 2013 at the age of 22 and has achieved the highest rating in the history of chess. This Norwegian Grandmaster has won all the top tournaments in the chess calendar, as well as the World Rapid Chess Championship, the World Blitz Chess Championship, and the ultimate prize in the chess world—the Classical World Championship title. In July 2022, Carlsen announced that he would not be taking part in the next World Championship match in order to concentrate on his regular tournament games. Despite that, he is, by far the number 1 ranked player in the world. His media-friendly persona has led to a massive growth in chess playing worldwide and has made Carlsen a global superstar.

CARLSEN'S CHESS STYLE

In his youth, Magnus Carlsen was described as "The Mozart of Chess" for his prodigious talent and the elegance with which he despatched his opponents. Carlsen enjoys sport, particularly soccer, and is exceptionally physically fit. This enables him to maintain his concentration at the chess board. He is renowned for playing out long games, persisting in trying to win in situations that others might abandon as a draw. In recent years he has developed his playing style after training with advanced machine-learning computers. He is more willing to give up pieces in order to directly attack his opponent's king.

> "Without the element of enjoyment, it is not worth trying to excel at anything."
>
> Magnus Carlsen

BUSINESS INTERESTS

Magnus Carlsen has proved that he is a winner off the chess board as well as on it. He helped to develop the Play Magnus app, which allows users to play a chess computer at different levels, matching Carlsen's strength at different ages.

A global celebrity, Carlsen has attracted sponsorship from many companies, appearing in advertisements for luxury cars, clothing, and sportswear brands, as well communications companies. In 2023 Puma launched a Magnus Carlsen branded sneaker "as a tribute to the game of chess."

> **"I spend hours playing chess because I find it so much fun. The day it stops being fun is the day I give up."**
>
> Magnus Carlsen

2016 WORLD CHAMPIONSHIP TIE BREAK

1 This was the spectacular final position of the final game. Carlsen (White) has just checked the king with the queen. Karjakin (Black) can take the queen in two different ways but both lead to checkmate.

2 If the king captures (**1...Kxh6**) then the rook slides over into the corner to deliver mate (**2 Rh8** checkmate).

3 If the pawn takes (**1...gxh6**) then the other rook moves down to take the pawn and again, the king has no way out (**2 Rxf7** checkmate).

CARLSEN'S CAREER

1990 Born in Tønsberg, Norway

1995 His father teaches him the rules of chess

1999 Participated in his first tournament, a low division of the Norwegian Chess Championship

2000 Receives coaching at the Norwegian College of Elite Sport by Norwegian Grandmasters and makes rapid progress

2003 Takes a year out of school to travel around Europe playing international chess tournaments

2004 Achieves the Grandmaster title and holds chess legend Garry Kasparov to a draw

2009 Wins the annual World Blitz Chess Championship for the first time

2010 Reaches no.1 in the world rankings

2013 Defeats Viswanathan Anand to become the classical World Chess Champion

2014 Beats Anand again to retain World title; wins the annual World Rapid Chess Championship for the first time

2016 Defends World title by defeating Sergey Karjakin

2018 Defeats Fabiano Caruana to retain World title

2020 Becomes the highest earning esports player in the world

2021 Retains World title with convincing victory over Ian Nepomniachtchi

2022 Wins the renowned Tata Steel Chess tournament for a record eighth time; Carlsen maintains his position as no.1 in the world rankings, but declines to play another world championship match

THE SHORTEST AND LONGEST GAMES

A game of chess can be decided in just a few moves—or it might take hundreds. And the play can be as quick or as slow as the players wish. One of the most popular forms of chess is "blitz" where both players have just a few minutes to make all their moves. And for some players even that isn't fast enough . . .

THE SHORTEST GAMES

The quickest checkmate can be achieved in just two moves—but only with a hugely cooperative opponent, so don't get your hopes up. It is no wonder that this checkmate is called Fool's Mate (**diagram 1**).

1 **1 g4 e5 2 f3 Qh4** Checkmate. The king, boxed in by its own pieces, has no escape. Terrible play from White! At the start of the game pawns should always be advanced from the center of the board, not from the side.

A quick checkmate that is more useful to know about is Scholar's Mate. This attack is not recommended—it can rebound horribly—but you should be aware of it in case someone springs it on you (**diagrams 2, 3, and 4**).

2 **1 e4 e5 2 Bc4** Sensible opening moves from both sides so far. The pawns advance in the middle and the bishop arrives at a good square. **2...Bc5 3 Qh5**

3 Black also plays the bishop out and White brings the queen into the game, threatening the pawn on **e5** and checkmate on **f7**. If Black moves the queen to **e7** both threats would be covered. But instead, Black makes a poor move: **3...Nc6 4 Qxf7**

4 Checkmate. Black spotted that the e-pawn needed to be defended and covered it with the knight, but missed the bigger threat—checkmate on **f7**. The Black king cannot take the queen because it's supported by the bishop. A checkmate that could have been avoided.

Magnus Carlsen has a reputation for playing long games, remorselessly wearing down his opponents, often with just a few pieces remaining on the board. He is renowned as the greatest endgame player in the world.

THE LONGEST GAME

Most modern tournament games take, on average, three to four hours to play, but can go on longer. In the 2021 World Championship match between Magnus Carlsen and Ian Nepomniachtchi, one of the games lasted a gruelling 8 hours without a break and took 136 moves. Nepomniachtchi lost that game and was so devastated that he never recovered in the match. But this is not the record. In 1989, a game played in serious competition lasted 20 hours and 15 minutes and took 269 moves. The result? A draw. Chess at the top level can be just as tough as other sports, which is why professionals nowadays take their physical condition very seriously.

THE MOSCOW MARATHON

The longest World Championship final took place in Moscow during 1984–1985 and involved the two Soviet players, Garry Kasparov (left) and Anatoly Karpov (right). The first to win six games would be declared the winner. However, after winning five games, Karpov was unable to finish off Kasparov. At one point, there were 17 draws in a row. The Russian chess public lost patience at one point, booing and wolf-whistling the two players.

Eventually, after a gruelling five months and 48 games, the match was abandoned by the President of the World Chess Federation, with Karpov suffering from physical and mental exhaustion. It is the only match in the history of the world championships to be abandoned without a result.

In the return match, later in 1985, a maximum limit of 24 games was re-introduced, much to everyone's relief.

Kasparov won the restarted match, describing the dramatic finale as the game of his life.

SPEED CHESS

If you don't want your match to last for months, try your hand at "bullet chess." The rules are simple—you have to play ALL your moves in one minute or you lose the game. You can play this frantic version of chess at websites such as LiChess.org, Chess.com and ChessClub.com.

SHAKERS AND RULE BREAKERS

Such are the passions aroused by chess that, occasionally, some players even break the rules in order to win. However, much more common than outright cheating is "gamesmanship." This is the art of unsettling your opponent, but staying within the rules of the game. As long ago as 1561, Ruy Lopez, one of the best players of his age, suggested positioning the board so that the sun shines in your opponent's eyes.

During the 1978 World Championship final, Viktor Korchnoi (left) alleged that Anatoly Karpov's team employed underhanded tactics.

UNSPORTING BEHAVIOR

A fairly common tactic is for a player to develop certain exaggerated mannerisms at the board. You might recognize the following types.

The **piece-thumper** will smash a piece down right in the heart of your army, hoping to convince you of its strength, even though their position might be poor.

The **smug opponent** will cast a bemused look at your move, and follow with a quick reply and an amused smile.

The **starer** is more intimidating. World Champion Mikhail Tal's penetrating stare unnerved one opponent so much that he countered by wearing reflective sunglasses.

The **table-shaker** can be equally unsettling. It is difficult to concentrate properly when the pieces are wobbling. The former World Champion, Tigran Petrosian, used this tactic against Viktor Korchnoi in 1977. Korchnoi asked him to stop, but Petrosian responded by turning off his hearing aid. Korchnoi replied with a swift kick. For the next game a partition was built under the table.

PUSHING THE LIMITS

The chess match that inspired the most gamesmanship was the 1978 World Championship final between Anatoly Karpov, representing the Soviet Union, and Viktor Korchnoi, who at that time was stateless. Korchnoi had defected from the Soviet Union two years earlier. Under such politically charged circumstances, there was always going to be enormous tension during the match.

In the middle of the second game, Karpov was handed a yogurt. Korchnoi's camp issued a formal protest after the game, claiming that the delivery could convey a coded message: "A yogurt after move 20 could signify 'We instruct you to offer a draw.' The possibilities are limitless." After this, it was decreed that Karpov could only have a particular flavor of yogurt and that it should be served at a specific time by a designated waiter.

A Soviet parapsychologist, Dr. Vladimir Zukhar, sat at the front of the audience staring directly at Korchnoi for the entire game. One of Korchnoi's delegation counteracted this by handing Dr. Zukhar a copy of the anti-Soviet novel *The Gulag Archipelago*, then sat behind him for the rest of the game prodding him with a ballpoint pen.

For the record, Karpov won the match.

In 1977, the Soviet player Tigran Petrosian had a bruising encounter with Viktor Korchnoi, involving table-shaking and the use of feet!

SMART PHONES

Cheating in the digital age has, sadly, become more common. Anyone can access a simple app on their phone that will play as well as the World Champion. It doesn't take too much subterfuge to slip out of the tournament hall, consult the phone and replay the computer moves on returning to the board. That's why, in most serious tournaments, players are required to hand over their phones to the referee and undergo airport-style security checks before play starts.

One of the most notorious scandals in top-level chess was the so-called "Toiletgate" World Championship match of 2006. Veselin Topalov (Bulgaria) was upset that his opponent, Vladimir Kramnik (Russia), was taking too many bathroom breaks and accused him of consulting a computer. A bitter dispute broke out and the match was temporarily suspended while an investigation took place. Nothing of note was discovered backstage and the match continued, though neither player was satisfied. Were the accusations simply psychological warfare?

CHEATING ONLINE

Online chess has created the opportunity for people to play from every corner of the globe, but has given rise to new difficulties. With no one watching, some unscrupulous players use computer assistance—and risk ruining their reputation. To counter this, most chess websites have introduced software that recognizes if someone with a low rating is playing too well. In other words, if they are using a chess computer to play stronger moves. Such cheats are banned from competitions. In the top online tournaments, to make absolutely sure that everyone sticks to the rules, players are observed by referees using two separate cameras.

WOMEN'S CHAMPIONSHIPS

The vast majority of chess tournaments are open to all, but there are some events for women only. For example, there are Women's World Championships in Classical, Blitz, and Rapid chess, and the Women's Chess Olympiad.

A GAME OF EQUALITY?

Despite the queen being the most powerful chess piece, there are far fewer women on the chess circuit. There have only been three women ranked in the world's top 100 players, with only Judit Polgar breaking into the top 10.

Arguments for this imbalance have been varied and include societal pressure taking its toll on women, a lack of possible confidence, and experiences of sexism at tournaments. Indeed, some of the best chess players have been dismissive of women's skills on the board.

Two of the greatest female players—Hou Yifan and Judit Polgar—have played in very few women's tournaments. Polgar stated that: "It is high time to consider the consequences of this segregation—because in the end, our goal must be that women and men compete with one another on an equal footing."

Others argue that the prize money and sponsorship available in women's tournaments can help them become professionals and will ultimately raise standards. The number of internationally rated female players is increasing and with hit shows such as The Queen's Gambit (see page 57) we may see numbers rise even more.

WOMEN'S CHESS OLYMPIAD 2022

The 44th Chess Olympiad was held in the summer of 2022, in Chennai, India. A record number of 161 teams took part in the women's event and the competition was fierce. The Indian team led throughout but were beaten in the final round, allowing Ukraine and Georgia to overtake them. Ukraine took the gold medals on tie-break with an unbeaten match record, and Georgia the silver medals. There were some brilliant individual performances. Pia Cramling won the gold medal for best result on board 1—repeating the award she first won in 1984. Polish player Oliwia Kiołbasa won nine consecutive games and achieved the highest rating performance in the event. The youngest participant in the Olympiad was eight-year-old Randa Seder of Palestine, who won her second-round game, sparking a media sensation.

With two former women's world champions on the team—Anna Ushenina and Mariya Muzychuk—Ukraine had an outstanding line-up. It was an emotional moment when the team was awarded with the gold medals.

THE GREATEST FEMALE PLAYERS

Judit Polgar is arguably the strongest woman ever to play professionally. At her best, she was among the top ten players in the world and a candidate for the world title.

One of her greatest achievements was beating the no.1 player in the world, Garry Kasparov, in 2002. Kasparov once said of Polgar: "She has fantastic chess talent, but she is, after all, a woman . . .no woman can sustain a prolonged battle." He came to regret these words.

Over the past few years, the highest rated woman chess player in the world has been Hou Yifan from China. She won the Women's World Championship on four occasions and in 2022 was the only woman in the world's top one hundred players.

She has preferred to concentrate on her academic career, becoming a professor at Shenzhen University in China.

In recent years, Yifan has declined to play in women-only tournaments, as she felt it was limiting her ambitions.

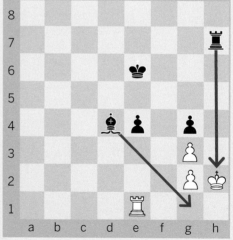

Polgar vs. Kasparov 2002

White's (Polgar) rooks dominate the seventh rank making it impossible for the king to escape. Before Polgar could swipe another pawn with the rook, Kasparov resigned the game, realising that his situation was hopeless.

YOUNGEST CHAMPION

Bibisara Assaubayeva from Kazakhstan became the youngest ever Women's Blitz Chess World Champion in 2021, at the age of 17. Her chess journey began when she played her first game with her grandfather at the age of 4, before going on to win the World Youth Championships in the girls under-8 category in 2011. In 2019, she joined the Kazakhstan national team at the Women's World Team Championship. Assaubayeva holds the titles of International Master and Woman Grandmaster.

At the Chennai Olympiad 2022, Assaubayeva played on board 2 for the Kazakhstan team and scored an unbeaten 8/11.

Vaishali vs. Assaubayeva, World Blitz 2021

Assaubayeva's rook (Black) has swept over to the side of the board, attacking the white king. The king cannot step out of the check as the escape square is covered by the bishop. Checkmate, and game over.

GREAT GAINS

In the past, Russia and other eastern European countries have produced the strongest chess players in the world. But over the last couple of decades, two nations have emerged as rising chess super-powers: India and China.

INDIA'S BOOM

India's chess boom has been inspired by the spectacular success of one player, Viswanathan Anand. He became the undisputed Classical World Champion in 2007 and subsequently defended his title in 2008, 2010 and 2012. He was also World Rapid Chess Champion in 2003 and 2017 and World Blitz Chess Champion in 2000. He was named Indian Sportsman of the year in 1991–92 and was awarded the second highest civilian honour in India, the Padma Vibhushan, in 2007.

Following Anand's example, millions now play the game seriously, particularly the younger generation, and from that base, strong players are emerging.

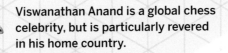

Viswanathan Anand is a global chess celebrity, but is particularly revered in his home country.

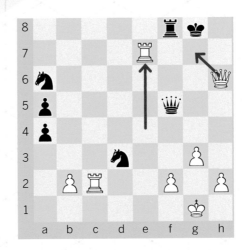

Anand—Topalov, World Championship Match 2010

This is one of Anand's most crushing and beautiful victories. He has just slammed the rook down the board, ready to support the queen in checkmating the hapless king. Topalov can only delay the finish, but not prevent it, so he resigned the game.

CHINA SUCCESS

China's success has materialized in a different way. There is less of a tradition of chess than in India and therefore fewer players. The massive improvement in the level of Chinese players is very much due to the targeted support of the government who helped to establish a national chess center in the country's capital, Beijing. Young talents are scouted and then given intensive coaching.

Ju Wenjun became the Women's World Chess Champion for the fourth time in 2023. China has dominated the Women's World title with no less than six champions in the past thirty years.

It could be argued that China has been more successful individually, but India is catching up. There are significantly more Indian players and this weight in numbers is leading to more and more breakthroughs, particularly in junior events. In the online Rapid Chess Olympiads during the COVID-19 pandemic, India triumphed.

China's World Champion

Ding Liren captured the ultimate prize by defeating the Russian, Ian Nepomniachtchi, in a tense match in 2023. After 14 classical games the scores were level. The first three games of the Rapid-play tie-break were drawn, then Ding won the fourth game, confounding the experts with a daring winning attempt.

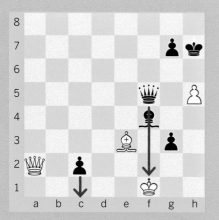

In the final position, White's king is exposed to checks and Black's pawn on c2 is about to advance to become a new queen. Nepomniachtchi resigned the game before Ding had a chance to checkmate him.

Afterward, Ding revealed how the intense pressure of the games had affected him: "This match reflects the deepness of my soul . . . I will cry. I will burst into tears. It was quite a tough tournament for me. I feel quite relieved."

Compare the two countries: which one will win out in future decades?
*correct as of 2023

INDIA

Highest ranked player:
Viswanathan Anand
Highest ranked woman:
Humpy Koneru
82 Grandmasters
Active internationally rated players: 10,943
Players in the top 100: 9
Players in the top 100 juniors: 18
Best position in the Classical Chess Olympiad: third in 2022
Online Rapid Chess Olympiad 2020: winners
Online Rapid Chess Olympiad 2021: second

Players from India won nine medals at the 2022 Chess Olympiad, including a first medal in the women's team event.

CHINA

Highest ranked player:
Ding Liren
Highest ranked woman:
Hou Yifan
49 Grandmasters
Active internationally rated players: 505
Players in the top 100: 9
Players in the top 100 juniors: 1
Best position in the Chess Olympiad: winners in 2014 and 2018
Online Rapid Chess Olympiad 2020: knocked out in the preliminaries
Online Rapid Chess Olympiad 2021: beaten in the semi-final

MAN VERSUS MACHINE

Since the pioneering days of computer science in the 1940s, researchers have developed and constructed chess-playing machines. The ultimate goal was for a computer to beat the strongest human chess player, although it took many decades to even threaten this. Finally, in May 1997, a chess match took place that would make headlines all over the world.

KASPAROV VERSUS DEEP BLUE

Garry Kasparov, at that time the reigning World Chess Champion, sat down to face *Deep Blue*, a 1.4-ton computer built and operated by a team of U.S. scientists funded by IBM, one of the world's largest computing firms.

The year before, Kasparov had convincingly defeated *Deep Blue*, and he was confident of success: "I don't think it is an appropriate thing to discuss whether I might lose. I never lose. I have never lost in my life."

"If a computer can beat the World Champion, a computer can read the best books in the world, can write the best plays, and can know everything about history and literature and people."

Garry Kasparov, World Chess Champion 1985–2000

As the match progressed it became clear that *Deep Blue* was far stronger than in previous years. Going into the sixth and final game, the scores were even. And then for the first time in his career, Kasparov cracked up. After just one hour—an average game at the top level of chess lasts about four hours—his position lay in ruins.

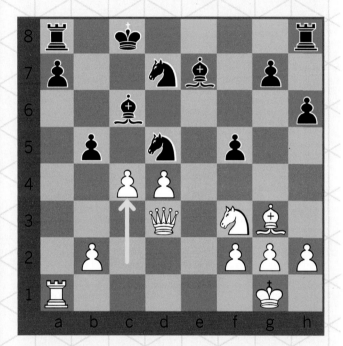

Kasparov (Black) has lost his most powerful piece, the queen. His king has been left exposed and is about to be cut down by *Deep Blue's* pieces. At this point, the human World Champion had had enough. He resigned the game.

At the closing ceremony Kasparov was livid. He raged that if *Deep Blue* were to play in a regular tournament, he would "tear it to pieces." Unfortunately for Kasparov, the *Deep Blue* team was disbanded after the match. The game was over: the best chess-playing computers were officially better than the best human players. But that wasn't the end of the story of computers and chess.

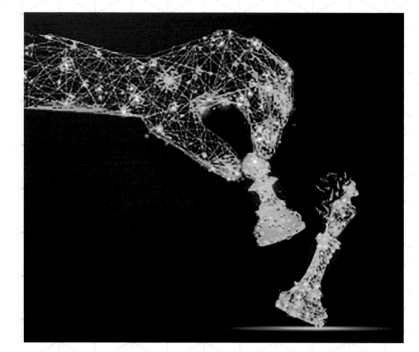

THE AGE OF ALPHAZERO

In 2017 Google's DeepMind team used ground-breaking technology to develop a new chess-playing machine, *AlphaZero*. The basic rules of chess were given to *AlphaZero*, which then played millions games against itself, evaluating how it could improve each time. In just a few hours it developed from an absolute beginner into the greatest chess-playing entity, capable of beating the strongest traditional chess software.

This was a massive scientific breakthrough. Professional players were in awe of *AlphaZero's* strength and its style. It was often prepared to give up pieces for activity, a complete change from previous computers and a style that influenced top professional players. Magnus Carlsen declared: "In essence I have become a very different player in terms of style than I was a bit earlier, and it has been a great ride."

The aims of the DeepMind team are far higher than just "solving" chess. Demis Hassabis, the lead scientist behind *AlphaZero*, declared: "We want to solve intelligence and then we use it to solve everything else." DeepMind have already used machine-learning technology to tackle complex medical problems, improve energy efficiency, and analyse climate change.

ESPORTS, TWITCH, AND YOUTUBE

When the COVID-19 pandemic of 2020 hit the world, the chess community suffered. Practically overnight, traditional chess activity stopped and the World Championship Candidates tournament was suspended halfway through and only resumed the following year. The chess calendar is normally very full for both amateurs and professionals, and there was huge demand to keep playing. A change was about to take place.

With players unable to meet, esports tournaments and matches became more important. Top professionals were attracted by big prize funds and spectators across the globe were eager for entertainment. Magnus Carlsen's company organised a series of Rapid Chess tournaments broadcast online.

Celebrities from the world of gaming and social media played in online "Pogchamps" championships, with expert chess players such as Danny Rensch and Alexandra Botez providing coaching and commentary for the games. The game of chess rapidly spun into a new era and chess players themselves became online celebrities.

Hikaru Nakamura, one of the strongest chess players in the world, has more than 1.5 million followers on his Twitch stream. He regularly plays Blitz chess and since the start of 2020, he has played hardly any face-to-face chess.

In the past, there was a clear recipe for chess improvement: find plenty of local competition, study books and secure a good teacher. Not everyone had these opportunities, but nowadays all this and more is available online. At the best chess websites, you can play games against humans or computers, join in with chess streamers, listen to commentary on the latest tournaments, read the latest chess news, solve puzzles, and watch instructional videos.

Popular sites on channels such as YouTube receive over one million subscribers. Each has a different style of presentation and most of the videos are free to view. As well as examining games by the leading players in the world there are also classic games from the past—a great way to learn about strategy.

"Because of the Internet, chess is not about your nationality or your background."

Hikaru Nakamura

International Master Anna Rudolf is a full-time chess streamer and commentator. Her Twitch and YouTube channels have received millions of views, making Anna one of the most popular online chess celebrities.

THE QUEEN'S GAMBIT

The most successful Netflix series of 2020 was The Queen's Gambit, the story of a fictitious chess player, Beth Harmon, who against all odds succeeds in a male-dominated world. The series coincided with the massive interest in chess during the COVID-19 pandemic, and inspired many women to learn how to play the game. Beth is an orphan and struggles to connect with people —until she is taught the game of chess. This becomes her passion and she progresses through the ranks, competing in junior tournaments, senior tournaments, the USA championship, and finally top international events, playing out her dreams.

The Queen's Gambit is one of the most popular chess openings. White gives up a pawn in order to conquer the center.

GLOSSARY

The following pages contain some of the more common terms used in chess. Not all of these terms are used in this book, but they may be useful if you read other books on the subject.

Blindfold chess A game in which the player cannot see the board—it isn't absolutely necessary to wear a blindfold! Players visualize the positions in their heads and call out their moves using chess notation.

Blitz chess Games played at a fast time control, usually less than 5 minutes for all moves. If played with an increment, then time is added each time a move is made, usually 2 seconds.

Bullet chess Games played with a time control of one minute for all moves. Hyper-bullet chess is even faster: 30 seconds for all moves

Check A piece that directly attacks the king is said to "give check" or put it "in check."

Checkmate The end of the game, when the king is put in check and cannot escape.

Combination A sequence of moves leading to material gain or checkmate.

Development Bringing pieces out at the start of the game. Having a "lead in development" can be of crucial importance.

Diagonal A line of squares running obliquely (on an angle) across the board, along which both the bishop and the queen are able to move. Diagonals are identified by naming the squares at either end, for instance, the b1-h7 diagonal.

Discovered check When a piece moves, allowing a second piece to give check.

Double attack One piece attacks two pieces at the same time. A knight fork is an example of a double attack.

Double check Two pieces put the king in check at the same time. This occurs when a discovered check is played and both pieces give check.

Endgame or Ending The third phase of the game, after the opening and the middlegame, when just a few pieces remain on the board. Strategy is different from the first two phases. For instance, mating attacks are rare, so the king becomes a powerful piece. Ultimately, the aim is to force a pawn to the eighth rank to get a new queen.

En prise A piece that is attacked but isn't defended is said to be "en prise." Similarly, a piece that is attacked by one less valuable than itself is also "en prise," for example, when a knight attacks a queen. ("Prise" rhymes with "cheese.")

Exchange, an When pieces of equal value are traded off the board. For instance, "a bishop exchange" means that both sides have given up a bishop. (Note that this is different from "the exchange," see below.)

Exchange, the This is a trade of particular pieces—a rook for a knight, or a rook for a bishop. If one player has lost a rook or a knight, for example, they are said to be "the exchange down."

Fianchetto The knight's pawn is advanced one square, creating room for the bishop to move on the longest diagonal—on g2 or b2 if you are White, b7 or g7 if you are Black. Although it is at the side of the board, the bishop influences the entire board.

FIDE (Fédération Internationale des Échecs) The world's governing body for chess, founded in 1924 in Paris. FIDE has many responsibilities. It determines the more obscure rules of the game, awards titles such as Master and Grandmaster, and hosts the chess Olympics.

File A line of eight squares running up the board. These vertical columns are often referred to by a letter, for instance, "Black's rooks can enter the position down the c-file."

Flank One side of the board.

Fork When two enemy pieces are attacked by a single piece, usually a knight.

Gambit An opening in which material is given up to gain a lead in development. Usually this is a pawn or two, but sometimes a gambit can involve sacrificing a more important piece such as a knight or a bishop.

Grandmaster Next to World Champion, the highest title in chess. Of the millions of serious players in the world, there are just a few hundred who have been awarded the title "Grandmaster" from FIDE. The full title is actually "International Grandmaster," but this is not used very often.

International Master The next title down from Grandmaster.

Kingside The half of the board on which the king

stands at the beginning of the game. In other words, the right-hand side of the board from White's point of view. Even if the king moves away to the left, the kingside remains the half of the board where the king was standing at the beginning. (See Queenside.)

Major piece A queen or a rook.

Material A term for pieces, often used in a more general sense when discussing values. For example, "White loses material" means that White loses more pieces than Black.

Middlegame The second of the three phases of the game. All pieces have been developed,and the real battle has begun. (See Opening and Endgame.)

Minor piece A knight or a bishop.

Open file A file on which there are no pawns, making it possible for a rook or a queen to penetrate deep into the enemy position. Sometimes controlling the only "open file" is enough for a player to force a win.

Opening, an A planned system at the beginning of the game.

Opening, the The first phase of the game. Pieces are brought out and the king finds safety.

Passed pawn A pawn that

has no enemy pawn in front of it or on an adjacent file. Potentially, this gives the pawn a free run to the eighth rank, where it can become a queen.

Pin A piece is attacked but cannot move because a piece behind it, usually of greater value, would be taken.

Pre-move In online Blitz chess, where speed counts, it is possible to play a move before your opponent has taken their turn. Once your opponent moves, your move will be played instantly. But beware that you have anticipated your opponent's move correctly.

Problem A composed position with a set number of moves to force a win or a draw.

Promotion When a pawn reaches the eighth rank it may turn into any other piece—knight, bishop, rook, or queen. Because the queen is so powerful, other pieces are rarely selected.

Queenside The half of the board on which the queen stands at the start of the game—from White's point of view, the left-hand side of the board. Even if the queen moves to the other half of the board, the queenside remains the half of the board where the queen stood at the beginning of the game. (See Kingside.)

Rank The rows of squares that run across the board, denoted by the numbers 1 to 8.

Resignation A player, knowing that defeat is inevitable, gives up the game before checkmate occurs.

Sacrifice When material is given up in order to gain an advantage in the long run.

Score sheet The official document on which moves are recorded during a game. All tournament games must be recorded—it is part of the official rules of chess.

Simultaneous exhibition (or simul). An event in which a Grandmaster or expert takes on a number of weaker players at once. Usually up to 30 players are taken on, but the record is currently held by Iranian Grandmaster, Ehsan Ghaem Maghami, who played 604 players simultaneously in Tehran in 2011. He won 580, drew 16 and lost 8

Skewer When two pieces are attacked along the same line. Usually, the most valuable piece is attacked first. After this piece has moved, the piece of lesser value behind it is captured.

Stalemate When the player whose turn it is cannot make any legal moves but is not in check. The game ends as a draw.

Strategy Long-term planning.

Tactics This has a distinct meaning in chess. A tactic is a short-term operation, usually played to win material. The more common tactics have acquired

colorful names such as "skewer."

Tempo, tempi A unit of time expressed in terms of a move. For instance, if the queen advances, but then has to retreat on the next turn, it could be said that a tempo has been lost (one move). If several tempi have been lost, then several moves have been wasted.

Time trouble All serious tournament games are played within a time limit, using a special chess clock. The standard time limit for tournament games is 40 moves in 2 hours for each player, followed by another 20 moves in 1 hour if the game is unfinished. When players mishandle their time allocation and must make several moves quickly to reach the required number of moves, they are said to be "in time trouble" or "under time pressure." Some players are time pressure addicts, who seem able to move only with the rush of adrenaline that comes when the clock approaches zero hour.

Under-promotion When a pawn reaches the eighth rank, but a piece other than the queen is selected.

Zugzwang A German word meaning "compulsion to move." Occasionally a situation occurs in which any move will compromise the player's position. It would be better to "pass," but this is not allowed.

ANSWERS AND RESOURCES

ANSWERS TO PAGES 10–14

Page 10: The king can take either the knight on d6, the pawn on d7, or the rook on f8.

Page 11: The rook can capture either the pawn on d6, or the knight on c1.

Page 12: The bishop is only able to capture one piece: the pawn on a2.

Page 13: The queen can capture either the rook on e7, the knight on b6, or the pawn on f2.

Page 14: The knight can capture either the pawn on e3, the bishop on b4, or the rook on c7.

1 Black should promote to a queen with **1...e1(Q)**— which actually puts White in checkmate.

2 By far the best move is to play **1...Nxg3**, winning a bishop at no cost. It is illegal for White to capture the knight with the pawn—this would put the king in check from the bishop on b6.

CONTACT ADDRESSES

America's Foundation for Chess
https://firstmovechess.org/

Chess Federation of Canada
www.chess.ca

FIDE (World Chess Federation)
www.fide.com

National Scholastic Chess Foundation
www.nscfchess.org

U.S. Chess Federation
https://new.uschess.org/

THE INTERNET

There are many websites dedicated to playing chess, as well as other aspects of the game: news, opinion, tuition and online shops.

These are the top five most popular websites where you can find playing partners and much more:
www.chess.com
www.chess24.com
www.lichess.org
www.chessclub.com (The Internet Chess Club - ICC)
www.playchess.com

YouTubers are a great source of instruction and entertainment. The most popular, each with over a million subscribers, are Gotham Chess and Agadmator, as well as GM Hikaru, hosted by Grandmaster Hikaru Nakamura. Each has a different style of presentation – find the one that suits you – and most of the videos are free to view. As well as examining games by the leading players in the world, there are also classic games from the past, and that is a great way to learn about strategy.

3 The best way to meet the threat from White is to move the king away from the middle as quickly as possible by castling: **1...0–0**. Tucked behind the pawns, Black's king is quite safe.

4 White should capture the pawn in the middle with the bishop: **1 Bxd5**, exploiting the pin. If the bishop is captured **1...Bxd5**, then White takes the rook with **2 Rxa7**. If it isn't captured, then White will take the bishop on **b7**. In either case, White has a winning material advantage.

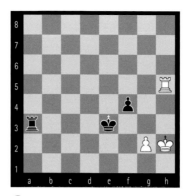

5 White can play **1 Rh3+**, skewering king and rook. Black's king must move, for instance: **1...Kf2**. White can then capture the rook on the other side of the board: **2 Rxa3**.

6 Black can checkmate in one move: **1...Qh2** mate.

7 White has a lethal discovered check: **1 Rf2+**. Black's king must move out of the check from the bishop: **1...Kg8**, then White takes the queen, **2 Rxg2**, giving a decisive material advantage.

8 There is more than one good move here, but the best is to sacrifice the queen with **1 Qxc5+**. If Black plays **1...Qxc5**, then White delivers a crushing blow with **2 Bxa6** checkmate.

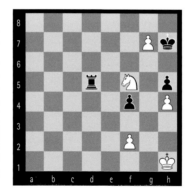

9 White has a very sneaky way to win from this position. White plays **1 g8(Q)+**. Black, of course, must capture the new queen: **1...Kxg8**, but then comes a knight fork: **2 Ne7+**. After Black's king moves out of check, the knight takes the rook. With an extra knight, White should be able to win the game.

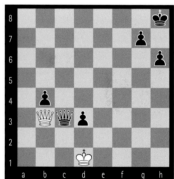

10 White can still draw the game with this amazing defence: **1 Qg8+**. Black must capture the queen, **1...Kxg8**, but then White has no legal move. As White is not in check, then the position is stalemate—a draw.

INDEX

ACKNOWLEDGEMENTS

The publishers would like to thank the following for supplying photographs:

Key: b = bottom, c = center, l=left, t = top, r = right.

4l UK Alan King/Alamy Stock Photo, 4b Gorodenkoff/Shutterstock; 5t & 5b CPA Media Pte Ltd/Alamy Stock Photo, 5r Interfoto/Alamy Stock Photo; 6tl Historic Collection/Alamy Stock Photo, 6tr Akkharat Jarusilawong/Shutterstock, 6cr Granger—Historical Picture Archive/Alamy Stock Photo, 6br ART Collection/Alamy Stock Photo; 7tr clu/Getty Images, 7cr Irina Wilhauk/Shutterstock, 7bl Marc Tielemans/Alamy Stock Photo, 7br New Africa/Shutterstock; 8–9 domin_domin/Getty Images; 8t Diana_Karch/Shutterstock; 43t Pauline Fox/Shutterstock; 44–45 Lilyana Vynogradova/Alamy Stock Photo; 48–49 Archive PL/Alamy Stock Photo; 48t Bettmann/Getty Images; 49r Andrey Mihaylov/Shutterstock; 52l dpa picture alliance archive/Alamy Stock Photo, 52br Sportsfan77777/Wikicommons; 54–55 Stan Honda/Getty Images; 54r Pictorial Press Ltd/Alamy Stock Photo; 57cl anttoniart/Shutterstock.

With kind thanks to Lennart Oates for permission to use images 47t, 50b, 51tr, 53b, 53r, 53t, 56bl.

With kind thanks to Anna Rudolf for the permission to use image 56br.

For Mairéad, Declan and Kit.